The Plant-based Vegan Recipes

50 HEALTHY VEGAN RECIPES DESIGNED FOR EVERYONE

Michael Nelson

All rights reserved.

Disclaimer

The information contained i is meant to serve as a comprehensive collection of strategies that the author of this eBook has done research about. Summaries, strategies, tips and tricks are only recommendation by the author, and reading this eBook will not guarantee that one's results will exactly mirror the author's results. The author of the eBook has made all reasonable effort to provide current and accurate information for the readers of the eBook. The author and it's associates will not be held liable for any unintentional error or omissions that may be found. The material in the eBook may include information by third parties. Third party materials comprise of opinions expressed by their owners. As such, the author of the eBook does not assume responsibility or liability for any third party material or opinions. Whether because of the progression of the internet, or the unforeseen changes in company policy and editorial submission guidelines, what is stated as fact at the time of this writing may become outdated or inapplicable later.

INTRODUCTION

WHAT EXACTLY DOES VEGAN MEAN?

The vegan diet is becoming increasingly popular. It is a sub-form of the vegetarian diet. As a reminder: vegetarians avoid meat, fish and seafood. A vegan also does without eggs, honey and dairy products. No animal foods are therefore consumed.

In addition, vegans are often forced to take a critical look at the ingredient lists of many foods. Animal ingredients such as lactose or gelatine can be found in a surprising number of products. Some fruit juices or beers are also clarified using gelatin. For this reason, these foods are also not vegan.

This change in diet may seem radical at first. After all, animal products are found in numerous foods and are simply part of a normal diet for many people. However, there is now a vegan substitute for almost every product with animal ingredients that can make the switch easier. However, these substitute products do not necessarily have to be lower in calories. The key to losing weight lies in the frequent use of unprocessed, fresh ingredients while avoiding animal foods. If you want to lose weight long-term and permanently and increase your chances of success, the vegan diet is exactly the right address.

Vegans eat only plant-based foods. You do without all animal products such as meat, fish, eggs, honey and dairy products.

VEGAN WEIGHT LOSS: DOES IT WORK?

More and more people are turning to the vegan diet to lose weight - and rightly so. Observational studies show that vegans have a lower body mass index (BMI) than non-vegans. The BMI has proven itself over the years as a measure for assessing a healthy body weight.

The plant-based diet is also superior to other forms of nutrition when it comes to weight loss. Numerous studies have shown that a low-fat, vegan diet caused the greatest fat loss among the diets compared.

In order to achieve success, vegans didn't even have to count calories. The study participants intuitively consumed fewer calories, but at the same time ate their fill with every meal. They were even able to lose more weight than the calorie-counting non-vegans in the comparison groups. Losing weight vegan seems to be a good way to get rid of a few annoying pounds.

It sounds almost too good to be true - always eat full and still shed the pounds. This is made possible by the high proportion of whole grain products, legumes as well as vegetables and fruit in a plant-based, vegan diet. Since these foods contain a lot of water and healthy fiber, they will fill you up for a long time while preventing food cravings. In addition, the complex carbohydrates in these foods provide the body with energy. The typical phases of tiredness that can often occur after a meal that is heavy on fat and meat do not occur.

In a direct comparison of the most common forms of nutrition, the plant-based diet suggested a low-meat and western diet in terms of weight loss for these reasons. Just doing without animal foods means a potential plus point for weight loss.

The vegan diet is usually lower in calories than other forms of nutrition. For this reason, it is ideal for losing weight healthily without constantly counting calories.

VEGAN WEIGHT LOSS: WHAT SHOULD I EAT?

Would you like to lose weight vegan but don't know what to eat and what not? We help you!

Eat a large amount of vegetables at every meal. Vegetables are high in fiber and contain a lot of water. Thus, it fills the stomach particularly well. At the same time, vegetables contain many vitamins and minerals that are essential for a healthy body. Since vegetables are almost fat-free and often low in carbohydrates, you should eat them without hesitation.

So that you get enough energy in your diet, you should focus on whole grains and legumes. Particularly healthy cereal products include oat flakes, whole meal pasta and fresh whole meal bread. Legumes include beans such as kidney and soybeans, as well as peas and lentils. Here are our most popular recipes with legumes:

Beans and Co. also provide plenty of healthy protein, which keeps you full for a long time and maintains muscle mass with regular exercise. In this way you protect your metabolism and counteract the yo-yo effect.

Also, avoid highly processed products. There are now many sweets and substitutes that do not contain animal ingredients. That makes them vegan, but by no means low in calories. If you want to lose weight vegan, your focus should be on unprocessed foods such as fruits, vegetables, nuts, seeds as well as grains and legumes.

Eat plenty of vegetables, whole grains, and beans to fill you up. On the other hand, avoid foods that are rich in fat and sugar.

Vegan foods high in calories

A good example of a vegan calorie bomb is vegan cheese. Of course, switching to a vegan diet is easier if the beloved Gauda is replaced with a cheese substitute instead of a vegan spread. However, many substitutes consist largely of fats such as palm or coconut oil. These fats are real calorie bombs.

When shopping, pay attention to the fat content and compare the calories that are in the nutritional table with animal products. Some meat substitutes, on the other hand, are even low in fat as they consist largely of soy protein. It is worth taking a look at the back of the product packaging.

The nut nougat cream in the morning, the cream for the kitchen, the chocolate in the evening and chips or biscuits are now also available in vegan versions. However, these do not have fewer calories than their representatives with milk and Co. .; so not suitable if you want to lose weight vegan. In addition to fat, sugar can also be a real fattener. Manufacturers often use so-called glucose-fructose syrup or is glucose to avoid the term sugar. These new types of sugar are even unhealthier than table sugar and whet the appetite a lot.

Avoid high-fat substitutes, as well as sweets and snacks. Be careful with products containing glucose-fructose syrup.

LOSE WEIGHT VEGAN: HOW TO COVER ALL NUTRIENTS

If you want to lose weight, you have to consume fewer calories than the body consumes. Only then does the body begin to draw the missing energy from the fat reserves. With such a reduction diet, the amount of nutrients such as minerals and vitamins supplied also decreases in the same breath. Since whole food groups are avoided, especially in the vegan diet, a well thought-out selection of foods is essential in order to counteract nutrient deficiencies in the long term.

For this reason, particularly nutrient-dense foods should be consumed. Remove high-calorie beverages as well as sugary desserts and snacks from your shopping list. White flour products such as bread rolls, toast or light pasta hardly provide any vitamins and minerals. Instead, opt for whole wheat bread or whole wheat pasta. Vegetables like broccoli, spinach or white cabbage provide a lot of nutrients and fill the stomach. This is the only way to successfully lose weight vegan.

Vegans should also eat legumes every day. Legumes like beans or lentils are among the best plant sources of iron. A helpful tip: combine legumes with foods rich in vitamin C such as fresh paprika and lemon juice, or have a kiwi for dessert.

Vitamin C increases iron absorption in the intestine and ensures an adequate supply. In order to absorb enough calcium, you have come to the right place with tofu, soy yoghurt or unsweetened soy milk.

As long as you eat a varied diet, avoid highly processed foods, and get most of your calories from grains, legumes, vegetables and fruits, your body should be adequately supplied with nutrients. The only exceptions are iodine and vitamin B12. Since iodine is only available in sufficient quantities in some types of algae and vitamin B12 is completely lacking in a vegan diet, these nutrients should be supplemented in the long term. You can find out more about vitamin B12 deficiency here.

LOSE WEIGHT FAST? HOW TO AVOID THE YO-YO EFFECT!

You may be familiar with the following scenario:

The decision has been made. You want to declare war on the kilos and are highly motivated. So get on the diet, welcome hunger, and focus on getting the scales steadily down. However, after a few weeks you will no longer have any strength. Your mood gets worse and worse and your thoughts revolve around the next meal. Worst of all, nothing happens on the scales. Now give up the diet and eat as before, the weight suddenly skyrockets and suddenly you weigh even more than before the diet. What did you do wrong?

Your body is very smart and, most importantly, efficient. As soon as he notices that he is no longer getting enough calories, he will try to reduce energy consumption. If you do not do much sport, the body breaks down "unimportant" muscles and puts the metabolism on the back burner.

As a result, your metabolism will gradually slow down until your body only uses as much as you eat in your diet. Suddenly the weight stagnates and you no longer lose weight. At the same time, you feel tired because your metabolism is in the basement. When you start to eat "normally" again, the body stays on the back burner for the time being and redirects the excess calories to the fat cells.

To avoid this, all you should do is eat five hundred fewer calories than you normally consume. You can also increase your activity by taking long walks, cycling or swimming. Weight training also sends signals to the body not to lose muscles. This is particularly important because the muscles consume a large part of the energy and thus the calories.

Once you have reached your desired weight, you will also have to recalculate your calories. Eat wrong and too much, slowly gain weight. Only by building up muscle mass can you get your metabolism going again. Try to keep all of this in mind if you want to lose weight vegan. Then nothing stands in the way of your desired weight!

Avoid a crash diet! With a deficit of 500 calories in combination with exercise, you will achieve your goal. Afterwards you should only eat in moderation.

A vegan, plant-based diet is particularly good for losing weight. No animal foods are used here. Meat and Co. are replaced with beans, lentils and other plant-based foods.

Thanks to the high consumption of voluminous and filling foods such as vegetables, whole grain products, legumes and fruit, you will stay full for a long time and you will not have to go hungry. In addition, these foods are rich in complex carbohydrates, which help you focus and give you the energy you need to get through your day.

Avoid crash diets and do not skip meals. Rather, rely on a combination of a small calorie deficit of five hundred calories and exercise to get fitter and leaner at the same time. Nobody needs to go hungry. With a well thought-out and wholesome vegan diet, you can shed those pesky pounds without weakening your body. Rather, the key is to stick with it for as long as possible and to give yourself and your body the time to get used to the new diet.

TABLE OF CONTENTS

CHICORY BOAT WITH SMOKED CROUTONS

Servings:2

INGREDIENTS

3 Tbsp olive oil

0.5 onion red, finely diced

250 ml Balsamic vinegar dark

1 Tbsp Raw cane sugar

 sea-salt at will

pepper at will

8 Tbsp Frying oil

200 G Smoked tofu finely diced

2 HeadsChicory

20th leaves young spinach

1 avocado ripe, finely diced

1 pear ripe, finely diced

PREPARATION

Heat the olive oil in a coated pan and sweat the onion cubes until translucent. Add the balsamic vinegar, sugar, a pinch of salt and a little pepper and let everything reduce at high temperature for 5–8 minutes, until about two thirds of the liquid has evaporated. Ventilate well, the evaporating vinegar stings your eyes easily. Make sure that not too much liquid evaporates in order to avoid burning or caramelizing too much. The reduction is always more fluid when it is warm than when it is cold. The smaller and more even the boiling sacs, the less liquid there is. Put some reduction on a cold plate as a test. If the reduction "stops", it is finished. Then take the pan off the stove.

Heat the frying oil in another pan and fry the tofu cubes at a high temperature for about 10 minutes until they are crispy and golden. The cubes should be crispy on the outside and juicy on the inside. Season to taste with salt and pepper.

Peel ten large leaves from the chicory heads and cleanly cut the broken edges. Divide the chicory boats on two plates and fill them with two spinach leaves and a couple of avocado and pear cubes.

Drizzle everything with a little balsamic reduction. Finally, fill each boat with tofu cubes. Arrange the remaining pear cubes and tofu croutons decoratively next to the boats on the plates and also drizzle with the reduction.

Recipe notes

Variation 1: The pear can be replaced by apple, apricot, grapes or cherries. Instead of spinach, rocket, lamb's lettuce, basil or Asian salads also taste good, and radicchio leaves can also be used instead of chicory. Variation 2: As a substitute for the tofu, roasted nuts, tempeh cubes or croutons made from bread, fried in olive oil with garlic until crispy and seasoned with salt and chilli are suitable.

CHILI SIN CARNE

Servings:4

INGREDIENTS

- 120 G Soy granules
- 500 ml Vegetable broth
- 3 Tbsp Rapeseed oil
- 2 Onions
- 4 G hot paprika powder
- 0.5 chili chopped
- 0.5 clove of garlic
- 50 G Tomato paste
- 1 Can tomatoes peeled off
- 250 G Kidney beans cooked
- 1 Can Corn cooked
- 1 TL salt
- 1 TL pepper
- 1 TL sugar

PREPARATION

Soak the soy granules in hot vegetable stock for 5-10 minutes, drain them and then fry them in a hot pan with rapeseed oil and the onion cubes. Briefly fry the paprika powder, chilli, garlic and tomato paste.

Add tomatoes, broth, kidney beans and corn and simmer for 20-25 minutes. Season to taste with salt, pepper and a little sugar. Bring to the boil again and serve.

Serve with bread or nachos.

VEGAN CROQUETTES MADE FROM COUSCOUS POTATO BATTER

Servings:4

INGREDIENTS

- 300 G   couscous
- 300 G   Potatoes cooked
- 1.5 TL   coriander ground
- parsley
- olive oil
- nutmeg
- salt at will
- pepper at will
- 50 ml   Lemon juice fresh
- 2 Tbsp Hazelnuts chopped
- 1.5 Tbsp Yeast fox
- rosemary fresh, at will

PREPARATION

Soak the couscous in water and then mix with the boiled potatoes and the other ingredients. Knead the dough until it has the desired consistency. Form croquettes out of it and bake in hot oil until golden brown.

It goes well with fried or steamed vegetables of the season.

Recipe notes

Tip: In addition to rosemary, other spices such as coriander and mint can also refine this dish. You can also add ground nuts to the dough as you like.

EGG-FREE SCRAMBLED TOFU EGGS

Servings:2

INGREDIENTS

- 1 onion
- 100 G   Smoked tofu
- 10 ml   Rapeseed oil
- 200 G   tofu nature
- 1 prize   turmeric
- 1 prize   salt
- 100 G   Silken tofu
- salt at will
- pepper at will
- 50 G chives

PREPARATION

Cut the onion into cubes and the smoked tofu into fine strips and lightly brown in a hot pan with oil.

Mash the natural tofu into fine pieces with a fork and mix with the turmeric and salt. Pour the mixture into the pan and fry until the tofu turns lightly brown.

Cut the silken tofu into large pieces and then fry briefly in the pan. Season to taste with salt and pepper, cut the chives into fine rolls and mix with the finished tofu scrambled eggs.

Recipe notes

Tip: The smoked tofu, which conjures up a hearty taste, and the silken tofu, which makes the tofu scrambled eggs nice and juicy, can be left out if they are not on hand. Turmeric should be handled very carefully, as too much turmeric makes the tofu scrambled eggs inedible and is mainly used to color it yellow.

VEGAN TUNA SANDWICH

Servings:4

INGREDIENTS

- Nori sheet Seaweed
- 60 G fine soy strips
- 2-3 gherkins
- 0.25 Federation parsley fresh
- 3 Tbsp mayonnaise
- 1 Tbsp Lemon juice
- 1 TL   mustard
- 0.25 TLpepper ground
- 0.5 TL coriander ground
- 0.25 TLcumin ground
- 0.25 TLPaprika powder
- 0.5 TL Fennel seeds ground
- 0.5 TL salt
- 8 Discs Wholegrain toast
- margarine
- 4 large lettuce leaves

- 1-2 tomatoes cut into thick slices

PREPARATION

Tear the nori sheet into small pieces and place in a bowl. Add soy shredded meat, pour boiling water over it and let it steep for 15 minutes. Then put everything in a sieve and lightly squeeze the soy shreds.

Chop the pickles, chop the parsley.

Briefly mix the soy strips and pieces of nori leaf with mayonnaise, pickles, parsley, lemon juice, mustard and all dry spices in a food processor or with a mixer. Transfer to a bowl, stir again and place in the refrigerator for at least 1 hour.

Spread the toast slices generously with margarine on one side. Heat a large pan over medium heat and fry the toast slices until golden brown.

Divide the "tuna" mixture into 4 slices, also distribute the lettuce leaves and tomato slices on top, close with the other slices, divide each diagonally and serve.

Recipe notes

Tip: If you want the "tuna" mixture to be warm, you can turn the finished sandwiches in the pan.

INDIAN LENTIL SOUP

Servings:4

INGREDIENTS

- 250 G   Yellow lentils
- 650 ml Vegetable broth for example from Alnatura
- 2 Carrots
- 1 Federation   coriander fresh
- 1 clove of garlic
- 2 TL salt
- 1 TL   turmeric
- 0.5 TL Curry powder
- 2 Msp. cumin ground
- 150 ml Soy cream optional

PREPARATION

Bring the lentils to the boil in the vegetable stock and simmer for
15 minutes over low heat with the lid closed.

Peel the carrots, dice finely and add to the lentils. Roughly chop the coriander and also add half. Peel the garlic clove and press finely. Season the soup with the pressed garlic, salt, turmeric, curry and cumin. Optionally pour in the soy cream. Let the soup simmer for another 5 minutes.

Now sprinkle the Indian lentil soup with the remaining chopped coriander and serve. Enjoy your meal!

VEGAN INDIAN STEW WITH GREEN PEAS

Servings:4

INGREDIENTS

- 500 G Potatoes
- 200 G aubergine
- 4 tomatoes
- onion
- 30 G   ginger fresh
- 0.5 Chilli pepper at will
- Sunflower oil for frying
- 1 Tbsp turmeric
- 1 TL Garam masala as desired (or spiced biscuits)
- 150 G tofu
- 150 G   green peas reveals
- salt at will
- 0.5 Federation   coriander fresh

PREPARATION

Peel, wash and dice the potatoes. Wash, clean, pat dry the aubergine and tomatoes and cut into cubes.

Peel the onion, peel the ginger root, dice both. Wash, clean, core and chop the chilli pepper. Then clean your hands well.

Mix the onion, ginger and chilli pepper and fry in a little oil over low heat.

Add the potato and aubergine pieces and season with turmeric and garam masala (or spiced biscuits). Sauté briefly and pour hot water over them so that the vegetables are covered. Let everything simmer for 5 minutes over low heat.

Add the tomatoes and simmer for 10 minutes.

Meanwhile, dice the tofu and fry until golden brown.

Add the green peas to the vegetables and finish cooking. Season to taste with salt.

Wash the coriander, shake dry and chop finely. Add the tofu pieces to the vegetable mixture just before serving and sprinkle everything with coriander.

Recipe notes

What goes with it? For example basmati rice with saffron. This combination not only looks beautiful, but also offers an abundance of flavors.

VEGAN STRAWBERRY ICE CREAM

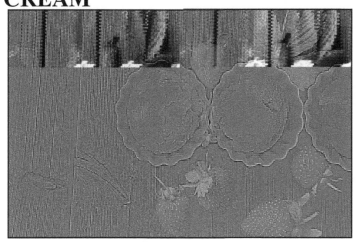

Servings:6

INGREDIENTS

- 500 G   Strawberries
- 1 Vanilla stick
- 300 G   (Soy) yogurt natural (alternatively vanilla or strawberry flavor)
- 2 Tbsp Agave syrup

PREPARATION

Clean and wash the strawberries. Cut 5 strawberries into small cubes and set aside. Cut the vanilla stick lengthways and scrape out the pulp.

Put all ingredients except the strawberry cubes in a blender and mix. Then fold in the cubes. Pour the ice cream mixture into a container and place in the freezer.

The ice should be frozen for about 5 hours. Meanwhile, stir the mixture vigorously every hour so that the ice cream becomes creamy. Just before serving, thaw a little and garnish with fresh strawberries.

VEGAN HERRING SALAD

Servings:2

INGREDIENTS

- 1 aubergine
- Lemon juice at will
- salt at will
- 1 Nori sheet Seaweed
- 1 Apples angry
- 2-3 Tubers Beetroot pre-cooked
- 1 small Red onion
- 5 gherkins
- 200 G   Soy yogurt unsweetened
- 2-3 Tbsp Pickle stock
- 1-2 TL dill rubbed
- pepper coarsely ground to taste
- 1 Tbsp neutral oil

PREPARATION

Peel the aubergine and cut lengthways into slices, then cut into pieces about 4 x 2 centimeters and lay out on a large wooden board. Drizzle both sides with lemon juice and season with salt. Then weigh down with another wooden board and a few books and let stand for at least 1 hour.

Tear the nori sheet into coarse strips and soak in water for at least 1 hour.

Finely dice the apple, beetroot, onion and pickles and fold into the yogurt. Take the nori seaweed out of the water, chop it finely and stir it into the mixture. Season with cucumber stock, dill, salt and pepper.

Dab the aubergine pieces well and then fry them with oil in a pan. Then let it cool down. Carefully add the cooled aubergine pieces to the yogurt mixture.

Recipe notes

Tip: Serve the vegan herring salad with bread.

GRILLED STRAWBERRIES WITH APPLE AND LAVENDER SORBET

Servings:4

INGREDIENTS

For the sorbet:

- 800 G   Apples sour
- 3 Tbsp Raw cane sugar fine, dark
- 4 Tbsp Apple sweetness
- 2 Tbsp Lime juice
- 2 Lavender branches
- 50 ml   water cold
- 250 ml Mineral water carbonated, cold

For the strawberries:

- 600 G   Strawberries
- 2 Tbsp powdered sugar
- 1 Tbsp Balsamic vinegar

Also:

- Aluminum foil
- Lavender flowers to decorate

PREPARATION

For the sorbet:

Peel and quarter the apples and cut out the core. Let the apple pieces, sugar, apple sweetness, lime juice, lavender sprigs and water simmer over a low flame for about 10 minutes. Take out the lavender.

Strain the apples finely with a hand blender and let them cool. Stir in the mineral water, place the sorbet mixture in the freezer and let it freeze for 3-5 hours, stirring occasionally.

For the strawberries:

Remove the leaves and stems from the strawberries. Halve or quarter the strawberries depending on the size. Then mix with the powdered sugar and balsamic vinegar. Wrap the strawberries in aluminum foil and place on the grill over medium heat for about 5 minutes.

Finally:

Take the strawberries out of the aluminum foil and place them in bowls. Spread the apple and lavender sorbet on top and garnish with a few lavender flowers.

VEGAN ONION LARD

Servings:1

INGREDIENTS

200 G   Coconut oil

1 onion medium-sized, finely chopped

3 Tbsp Hazelnuts chopped up

½ Apples sour, diced

1 TL salt

1 prize pepper

 Something Caraway powder

 Something Paprika powder

PREPARATION

Melt the coconut oil in a saucepan and steam the onion in it. Briefly sauté the rest of the ingredients and remove the saucepan from the heat. Season to taste and let cool down.

As soon as the mixture has solidified, beat well with a whisk or a spoon so that it becomes creamier. Fill into a large glass.

Recipe notes

The vegetable onion lard tastes delicious on bread.

MAKE SOY YOGURT YOURSELF

Servings:2

INGREDIENTS

- 500 ml soy milk
- 2 Tbsp Bread drink

PREPARATION

Heat the soy milk in the pot with a kitchen thermometer to 42 °
C (not hotter!) And stir in the bread drink. Pour the mixture into
a thermos and wrap it up warm so that the heat stays in place.
Let stand overnight and refrigerate the finished yoghurt the next
day. The thick, homemade yogurt is ready.

MAKE YOUR OWN FALAFEL WITH TAHINI SAUCE

Servings:4

INGREDIENTS

For the falafel:

- 100 G   Chickpeas
- 800 ml water cold
- 1 Bay leaf
- 1 TL salt plus a little more to taste
- ½ onion
- about 500 ml   olive oil
- clove of garlic
- Chilli pepper fresh
- ½ Federation parsley
- 50 G couscous
- 50 G Whole wheat flour

- 1 Tbsp Tahini (Sesame mushrooms; can be found in every supermarket, health food store and health food store.)
- 1 TL Lemon juice
- 1 TL cumin
- pepper black, freshly ground

For the tahini sauce:

- 100 G Tahini
- 1/2 clove of garlic
- salt at will
- pepper freshly ground to taste
- 100 ml water cold

PREPARATION

For the falafel:

Soak the chickpeas in 800 ml of water in a bowl for 24 hours.

The next day, bring the chickpeas together with the soaking water, the bay leaf and 1 teaspoon salt to a boil in a saucepan. Cook in a closed saucepan over low heat for about 1 hour. Pour off the boiling water, leaving 50 ml. Let the chickpeas cool down a bit, then puree them together with the remaining cooking water.

Peel the onion, chop it finely and fry it in a pan with 1-2 tablespoons of olive oil. Peel and squeeze the garlic. Fry briefly. Wash the chilli pepper, remove the stone and white partitions and finely chop the pod. Wash and finely chop the parsley. Pour 50 ml of boiling water over the couscous. Stir in 1 tbsp olive oil and a little salt. Let it steep for 10 minutes in a closed vessel.

Mix the chickpea puree, onion and garlic mixture, 1 pinch of chopped chilli pepper, parsley, couscous, flour, 1 tbsp tahini, lemon juice and cumin. Season to taste with salt and pepper.

Shape cams, medallions or balls out of the mass. Fry in the remaining olive oil (approx. 480 ml) over medium heat, bake in a pan with plenty of oil or bake in an oven preheated to 200 ° C on an oiled baking sheet until brown.

For the tahini sauce:

Peel and press the garlic clove. Puree all ingredients with 100 ml water with a hand blender or blender.

Recipe notes

This goes well with fresh salad, fried vegetables and pita (thin flatbread).

HEALTHY GREEN SMOOTHIE WITH TURMERIC AND GREEN VEGETABLES

Servings:3

INGREDIENTS

- 1 medium-sized cucumber
- 1 medium zucchini
- 3 Kohlrabi leaves
- 3 Beetroot leaves
- 1 Chard leaf
- ½ TL   ground turmeric or 1 cm from the turmeric tuber
- 1 TL   white peppercorns
- 3 Stalk coriander
- 350 ml water
- For the decoration:
- 3 thin zucchini slices
- 3 thin cucumber slices

PREPARATION

Wash and slice the cucumber and zucchini. Rinse the kohlrabi and beetroot leaves with cold water, drain and cut into small pieces. Separate the green from the chard, do not use the white stem, cut the rest into small pieces.

Peel and chop the turmeric tuber or put the turmeric powder in the blender along with the peppercorns and other ingredients. Add the water.

Start the mixer briefly on the lowest level, then puree everything on the highest level until a creamy smoothie is created. Check consistency and taste. Add a little more water or salt and pepper if you like and mix again briefly.

Pour smoothie into glasses. Cut the zucchini slices and the cucumber slices up to the middle and place them 1 cm apart on the edge of the glass. Serve fresh and enjoy.

Recipe notes

Info: Turmeric is a plant tuber that stimulates the production of bile and thus facilitates digestion, stimulates the immune system and has been proven to protect against tumors. As a natural antioxidant, turmeric delays the aging process in humans and makes food last longer.

VEGAN PASTA PAN

Servings:4

INGREDIENTS

- 500 G   Fleckerlnudeln alternatively: Farfalle or mussel noodles
- 5 Tbsp Rapeseed oil
- 300 G   Smoked tofu
- 1 onion large
- 250 G   Soy cream
- 4-5 Stems Marjoram leaves or thyme
- 1 Federation parsley
- 300 G   (Frozen) peas
- salt at will

PREPARATION

Boil the pasta in salted water until firm to the bite, drain and mix with 1 tablespoon of rapeseed oil so that the noodles do not stick together.

Cut the smoked tofu into small cubes. Peel and finely chop the onions. Fry both in 4 tablespoons of rapeseed oil, deglaze with 100 ml of water and the (soy) cream. Add chopped herbs, peas and salt. Let everything cook for 5 minutes on a low heat.

Fold the pasta into the sauce and serve.

Recipe notes

This goes well with green salad with rapeseed oil dressing.

WOK VEGETABLES WITH PEANUT SAUCE

Servings:4

INGREDIENTS

For the wok vegetables:

- 500 G   broccoli
- 1 Red onion
- 1 red pepper
- 250 G   Mushrooms
- 20 G   ginger
- 2 Garlic cloves
- 2 Tbsp peanut oil
- 2 Tbsp light soy sauce
- 2 TL   brown cane sugar
- salt at will

For the peanut sauce:

- 1 onion

- 1 clove of garlic
- 1 Tbsp   peanut oil
- 1 Tbsp   Red curry paste
- 1 Tbsp   Agave syrup
- 100 G   Peanut butter from the glass
- 200 ml   Coconut milk in a can
- 200 ml   Vegetable broth cold
- 1 TL   Lemon juice freshly pressed, possibly more
- salt at will

PREPARATION

For the wok vegetables:

For the vegetables, clean and wash the broccoli, remove the stem and cut the head into small florets. Cover and steam in a saucepan with a steamer over boiling water for about 5 minutes until al dente. Drain the broccoli in a colander, quench and allow to drain.

Peel the onion, cut in half lengthways and crossways and cut into thick slices. Halve the peppers lengthways, remove the seeds, wash and cut the halves into cubes. Clean the mushrooms, rub dry and cut in half or into slices. Put the ginger and grate. Peel and finely dice the garlic.

Heat the oil in a wok or high pan. Sear the bell pepper, mushrooms and onion in it. Add the broccoli, ginger and garlic and fry for another 2 minutes. Now add the soy sauce and sugar and season with the salt.

For the peanut sauce:

Peel and finely chop the onion and garlic. Heat the oil in a pan, fry the onion, garlic, curry paste and agave syrup in it for about 3 minutes.

Add the peanut butter, coconut milk, stock and lemon juice, bring to the boil and cook over low heat for about 5 minutes. Season the sauce with the salt and lemon juice.

Finally:

Divide the vegetables on plates and serve with the peanut sauce. Basmati rice or fried rice noodles are ideal as a side dish.

Recipe notes

If you like, you can also fry 50 g soybean sprouts and 2 tablespoons cashew nuts with the vegetables.

CORN SALAD WITH FIGS AND WALNUTS

Servings:4

INGREDIENTS

For the tofu:

- 150 G   tofu
- 4 Tbsp olive oil
- 3 Tbsp Lemon juice
- 1 Knife point Fennel seeds ground
- pepper at will
- salt at will
- olive oil to fry
- For the salad:
- 2 Fennel bulbs
- 4 Figs fresh or dried
- 1 Federation Lamb's lettuce
- 80 G Walnuts lightly toasted, roughly chopped

PREPARATION

For the tofu:

Squeeze the excess water out of the tofu and cut it into cubes.
Marinate these for about an hour in 2 tablespoons of olive oil, 3
tablespoons of lemon juice, a knife point of ground fennel seeds,
pepper and salt. Then remove from the marinade (be sure to
save) and fry in olive oil until golden brown.

For the salad:

Cut off the green of the fennel and peel the outermost leaves
with a peeler. Then cut the fennel into wafer-thin slices
(preferably with a vegetable slicer or a grater). Prepare a bowl of
ice water and add the fennel slices. Then let it rest for at least 15
minutes so that the fennel becomes crisp.

Peel the figs and cut into small pieces. Wash the lamb's lettuce
thoroughly and spin dry. Also spin the fennel dry and mix it with
the lettuce, fried tofu, figs and nuts. Pour the tofu marinade on
top and serve.

FRUIT SALAD À LA PROVENÇALE

Servings:4

INGREDIENTS

- 2 Honeydew melons
- 8 large apricots
- 12 Ears of real lavender

PREPARATION

Cut the honeydew melons, which should be as juicy and aromatic as possible, in half and remove the stones with a spoon.

Use a medium-sized ball cutter to cut even balls out of the pulp. Add the juice that forms in the melon halves to the salad later.

Core the apricots and cut into wedges. Mix this with the melon balls and the juice and fold in the stripped flowers of 8 lavender ears.

Arrange the salad in 4 bowls and decorate with 1 ear of lavender each.

OVEN VEGETABLES WITH ORANGE HUMMUS

Servings:4

INGREDIENTS

For the oven vegetables:

- 400 G Beetroot
- 400 G   Mandarin Pumpkin or parsnips
- 2 Potatoes
- 3 Carrots
- 2-3 Onions cut into stripes
- 4-5 Garlic cloves quartered
- olive oil for frying
- 1 lemon
- salt at will

For the orange hummus:

- 250 G Chickpeas from the can, drained
- 60 ml orange juice
- 40-55 G Tahini (Sesamus)
- 1 clove of garlic
- 1 Tbsp Lemon juice
- 1 Tbsp olive oil
- 1 orange untreated, peeled off from it
- ½ TL salt
- pepper from the mill, at will

PREPARATION

Preheat the oven to 200 ° C. Wash the beetroot thoroughly, remove the stalk at the top and bottom and cut the tubers into bite-sized pieces. Wash the pumpkin, core the unpeeled and cut into wedges. If parsnips are used, wash them and cut them into pieces without peeling. Wash the potatoes and carrots and cut into bite-sized pieces, unpeeled.

Spread the potatoes, beetroot, onions and garlic on a baking sheet. Spread olive oil over it. Cook the vegetables in the preheated oven for 40-45 minutes. After 10 minutes of baking, spread the carrots and parsnips, after 20 minutes the pumpkin wedges on the tray. Drizzle everything with olive oil again and finish baking until all the vegetables are soft.

Halve the lemon and squeeze over the vegetables. Salt the vegetables properly.

For the hummus, thoroughly puree all ingredients except the orange peel with the hand blender. Add the bowl and season the hummus with the salt and a little pepper.

Serve the vegetables with the hummus. Good bread goes well with it.

BAKED POTATOES WITH DIP AND SALAD

Servings:2

INGREDIENTS

For the baked potatoes and the pepper and tomato dip

- 2 200 g organic potatoes
- 1 Tbsp olive oil
- 1/2 onion chopped
- 2 Red pepper Stripes
- salt
- 100 ml sieved tomatos Tetra pack
- 1 Hot peppers fine rings
- For the fasting salad with grass green dressing
- 100 G   cucumber coarsely grated
- 8 leavesLettuce fine stripes
- 1 Federation parsley finely chopped
- 3 Tbsp Lemon juice
- 1 Tbsp olive oil

- salt and pepper
- 300 G   vegetables cut and grated
- 150 G   Leaf salads

PREPARATION

Wrap the potatoes in aluminum foil, fry them in the oven at 200 ° C (180 ° C hot air, gas mark 5) for about 50 to 60 minutes. Heat the olive oil for the dip. Steam the onion in it until soft. Add paprika, fry briefly, season with salt. Mix in the tomatoes and cook covered for about 10 minutes until the peppers are soft. Puree everything with the blender and season with salt. Cut the baked potatoes open, fill with the dip and sprinkle with hot peppers.

For the salad, puree the cucumber, lettuce, parsley, lemon juice and oil into a smooth dressing with a hand mixer, season with a little salt and pepper. Mix the salad ingredients that you put together according to the season and personal appetite with the dressing.

VEGAN CHRISTMAS ROAST MADE FROM CASHEW NUTS

Servings:6

INGREDIENTS

- 75 G Soy granules
- 200 ml water hot
- 250 G   Cashews
- 80 G   Almonds
- 40 G   Walnuts
- 2 Tbsp Egg substitute
- 8 Tbsp water cold
- 1 onion
- 1 carrot
- 2 Tbsp Frying oil
- 100 G   Breadcrumbs
- 40 G   Yeast flakes
- 2 Tbsp Tomato paste
- 300 ml Vegetable broth

- 1 Federation parsley fresh, crushed
- 1 onion
- 2 Tbsp Frying oil
- 150 G   tofu
- 50 ml   sesame oil
- 4 Tbsp Soy sauce
- 2 TL Dijon mustard
- 1 TL Maple syrup
- salt at will
- pepper at will

Also:

- Parchment paper

PREPARATION

Soak the soy granules in hot water for 10 minutes. Then squeeze the liquid out of the soy granulate. Chop cashew nuts, almonds and walnuts in a blender. Dissolve the egg substitute in water.

Chop the onion and grate the carrot. Fry both in oil.

Mix the crushed nuts, soy granules, half of the breadcrumbs and the yeast flakes in a bowl. Add the onion and carrot mixture, the dissolved egg substitute and the tomato paste. Pour the vegetable stock over them and mix everything into a dough. Season to taste with salt, pepper and a little parsley.

Line a loaf pan with baking paper so that the baking paper overlaps on the sides and the cashew roast can be easily lifted out of the pan after baking. Spread half of the nut mixture in the mold and smooth it out.

In the meantime, prepare the filling: cut the onion into cubes and fry in oil. Squeeze the liquid out of the tofu and crumble the tofu, add to the onion and fry for 3 minutes. Season to taste with salt, pepper and plenty of parsley. Sage or thyme can also be used instead of parsley.

Spread the filling in the middle of the mold. Pour the rest of the nut mixture over it so that the filling is covered on all sides.

Mix the sesame oil, soy sauce, Dijon mustard and maple syrup. Brush the vegan roast with half of the glaze.

8thBake in the oven at 175 ° C (top / bottom heat 190 ° C) for about 25 minutes, then distribute the rest of the glaze on the cashew roast, sprinkle the remaining breadcrumbs on top and bake for another 25 minutes.

Let the vegan Christmas roast cool down for 10 minutes before you can lift it out of the pan.

Recipe notes

Tip: Caramelized carrots, duchess potatoes, spicy cranberry sauce or winter vegetables such as leeks, kohlrabi and parsnips taste great as accompaniments to cashew roast. A delicious starter is lamb's lettuce with fried smoked tofu cubes and pomegranate seeds with agave syrup and mustard dressing.

FRESH GRAIN PORRIDGE

Servings: 1

INGREDIENTS

- 3 Tbsp any grain one or more varieties
- fruit to taste and appetite, crushed
- something   Lemon juice
- Nuts, seeds or kernels Almonds, hazelnuts, cashew nuts, para or macadamia nuts, whole or chopped
- Oilseeds z. B. sunflower seeds, flax seeds, sesame seeds, also in sprouted form
- ½ TL   cold pressed oil z. B. linseed oil

PREPARATION

Coarsely grind the grain with a flour mill, mixer or coffee grinder or squeeze it into flakes with the flaker. Mix the ground grain with cold water to a pulp and let it soak for five to twelve hours at room temperature.

Add fruit, lemon juice and, if necessary, nuts and oil seeds, stir in oil.

FRUITY AVOCADO SALAD

Servings:2

INGREDIENTS

- 2 Avocados ripe
- 2 Apples small
- 2 Red onions or shallots, small
- 2 Msp. paprika sweet
- salt at will
- pepper at will
- 4 Tbsp olive oil
- 4 Tbsp Lemon juice
- 1 TL vinegar

PREPARATION

Halve the avocados and remove the core. Use a teaspoon to remove the pulp from the skin in one piece and cut into small slices.

Wash the apples, cut eighths, remove the core and also cut into slices. Peel the onions and cut into half rings. Mix everything well in a bowl with paprika, salt and pepper, oil, lemon juice and vinegar and serve.

FRUITY RED CABBAGE SALAD

Servings:4

INGREDIENTS

- 50 G   Sultanas
- ½ Red cabbage
- onion medium-sized
- 1 prize Cloves ground
- ½ TL   cinnamon ground
- sea-salt at will
- black pepper freshly ground to taste
- Apples sour
- 1 orange
- 1 banana
- 50 G   Walnut kernels
- 2 TL   Rice syrup
- 6 Tbsp Sunflower oil
- ½ lemon of which the freshly squeezed juice
- 1 orange of which the freshly squeezed juice

PREPARATION

Soak the sultanas in warm water for about 30 minutes. In the meantime, remove the outer leaves from the red cabbage and cut or slice the rest very finely. Peel the onion and cut into fine cubes. Mix with the red cabbage in a bowl and season with ground cloves, cinnamon, salt and pepper.

Halve and core the apples and finely dice with the skin. Fillet the orange. To do this, peel the fruit so that the white skin is completely removed. Then cut the orange fillets out of the separating skin with a sharp knife and divide them into bite-sized pieces. Peel and slice the banana. Chop the walnut kernels.

Add the apple, orange and banana pieces with the walnut kernels, the drained sultanas, the rice syrup and the oil to the salad and mix everything carefully.

Pour the orange and lemon juice over the red cabbage salad, mix again, cover and let steep for at least 2 hours.

Before serving, mix the red cabbage salad again carefully and season with salt and pepper to taste. Fresh flatbread tastes good with it.

VEGAN ORANGE CAKE WITH GRID STRIPS

Servings: 1

INGREDIENTS

- 1 Springform pan

Dough:

- 200 G   margarine
- 200 G   sugar Full pipe
- 1 TL cinnamon
- untreated lemon Bowl
- 250 G   Wheat flour full grain
- 1 TL   baking powder
- 250 G   ground walnuts
- pinch of salt

Filling:

- ½ Glass Orange jam about 170 g

- For dusting:
- 1 Tbsp powdered sugar

PREPARATION

Beat margarine with sugar and cinnamon until creamy. Wash the lemon and rub the peel. Stir in the lemon zest, the flour mixed well with the baking powder, the ground walnuts and the salt.

Line a 28 cm diameter springform pan with two-thirds of the batter. Spread orange jam on top.

Roll out the remaining dough and cut into narrow strips. Lay these over the cake like a grid. Bake at 170 ° C for about 25-30 minutes.

Dust the slightly cooled cake with powdered sugar.

CRUNCHY KALE SALAD WITH YOGURT VINAIGRETTE

SERVINGS 4

INGREDIENTS

- Kale
- 1 bunch kale with stems removed
- ¼ cup olive oil
- ¼ teaspoon salt
- Yogurt Vinaigrette
- ¼ cup olive oil
- ¼ cup Greek vanilla yogurt
- 2 tablespoons red wine vinegar
- 1 tablespoon lemon juice

- 2 teaspoons coarse-grained Dijon mustard
- 1 teaspoon finely chopped garlic
- Topping
- ¼ cup oats 'n honey protein granola
- ¼ cup dried cranberries

PREPARATION

In a wide bowl, blend the kale, 1/4 of a cup of olive oil and salt. Massage the hands for 2 to 3 minutes or until they are gently softened by the kale.

Place the yogurt vinaigrette components in the blender or food processor. Cover; blend until smooth, or process it.

Divide the four plates of kale. Drizzle with vinaigrette, top with dried cranberries and granola. Move into the remainder of the dressing room.

VEGAN BACON & HERB WINGS

SERVINGS 4

INGREDIENTS

- 1 chicken, cut into 8 pieces, reserve wings for other use such as stock or soup, remove skin from the rest
- 4 cloves garlic, minced
- 1 fresh chile, such as Fresno chile, finely chopped
- About 2 tablespoons rosemary, very finely chopped
- About 2 tablespoons thyme, finely chopped
- Sea salt and coarsely ground pepper
- About 1/4 cup Virgin Olive Oil
- 6 fresh bay leaves
- 6 thin slices good quality bacon

PREPARATION

Put the chicken with the garlic, chili, rosemary and thyme in a dish. Season with sea salt carefully, and with pepper a little more. To coat the chicken parts with herbs and garlic, sprinkle the olive oil over the chicken and pour it evenly. Using or marinate directly overnight.

Preheat the oven to 375F. Over a baking sheet, organize a wire refrigerator rack.

Using small leg leaves to put the bay leaf on top of each chicken piece. Wrap around each chicken piece a slice of bacon so that each piece is partially exposed and the bay leaves a spot under the bacon.

On the rack, place your chicken. Bake until the bacon is crisp and the chicken is cooked through, for 45 minutes.

Serve with grilled asparagus or grilled tomato and corn salad and red onion...

BANANA-WALNUT STEEL CUT OATMEAL

SERVINGS 4

INGREDIENTS

- 4 cup(s) Water
- ¼ tsp, Table saltor to taste
- 1 cup(s) Uncooked steel cut oats
- 2 medium, Banana(s) ripe, mashed
- 1 Tbsp Packed brown sugar
- 2 tsp Unsalted butter
- ½ tsp Vanilla extract
- ¼ cup(s) Low-fat milk
- 8 tsp Chopped walnuts

PREPARATION

In a medium saucepan, bring the water and salt to a boil; stir in the oats and bring them to a boil. Reduce heat to low and simmer, uncovered, stirring occasionally, for about 25 to 30 minutes, until oats are tender; remove from heat.

Add the bananas, sugar, butter and vanilla and whisk in the milk. Serve the walnuts-garnished oatmeal.

Serving size: 1 cup of oatmeal and 2 tsp of walnuts, respectively.

In a medium saucepan, bring the water and salt to a boil; stir in the oats and bring them to a boil. Reduce heat to low and simmer, uncovered, stirring occasionally, for about 25 to 30 minutes, until oats are tender; remove from heat.

Add the bananas, sugar, butter and vanilla and whisk in the milk. Serve the walnuts-garnished oatmeal.

Serving size: 1 cup of oatmeal and 2 tsp of walnuts, respectively.

CAJUN SHRIMP AND GRITS

SERVINGS 4

INGREDIENTS

- 1 package Vegan Shrimp
- 5 oz. of Vegan Chorizo chopped
- 1/3 cup Red Bell Pepper
- 2 Green Onions sliced
- 2 cloves of Garlic minced
- 2 1/2 Tbsp. of Vegan Butter
- 3 Tbsp. of Water
- 1 tsp of Cajun Seasoning
- 1 tsp of Old Bay Seasoning
- Salt & Pepper to taste
- Creamy Grits

- 1 cup Organic Corn Grits
- 2 cups of Broth or Water
- 2 cups of Plant Milk
- 1/3 cup grated Vegan Chedar Cheese
- 1 Tbsp of Vegan Butter
- Salt & Pepper to taste

PREPARATION

In a large pot, bring the water and milk to a gentle boil. Add in the Corn Grits and mix well to ensure no lumps form. Reduce heat and simmer for 25 -30 minutes or so.

Place the cheddar with the cheese, butter, salt & pepper. Rarely, once the cheese has melted, stir. Cover and keep warm until the shrimp has been cooked.

In a pan, saute the chorizo and 1/2 tablespoon of butter until crisp. Retire and set aside.

In the same pan, melt 2 Tbsp of butter over medium-low heat. Garlic is added and, when fragrant, roasted. Apply the shrimp, Cajun and Old Bay seasonings, then cover and proceed to cook for 5-8 minutes.

In the chopped red pepper, add the white portions of the green onions and the water and continue cooking on medium for another 5 minutes. Put the cooked chorizo back into the shrimp and stir well.

Serve with the Shrimp & Chorizo mixture and garnish with Green Onions over a bowl of the Grits.

VEGAN BLUEBERRY MUFFINS

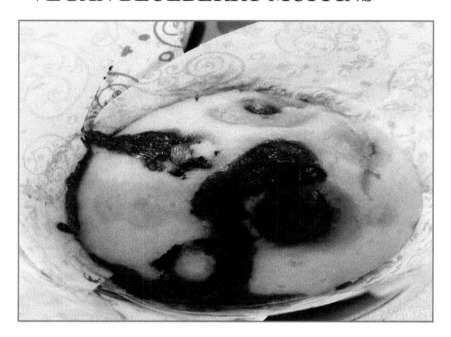

YIELD: MAKES 12 MUFFINS

INGREDIENTS

- 2 cups flour (all-purpose, spelt, white whole wheat or combo)
- 2 ½ teaspoons baking powder
- ¼ teaspoon mineral salt
- ¾ cup organic pure cane or turbinado sugar
- 1 cup unsweetened almond milk
- ⅓ cup olive oil (or fruit infused olive oil: lemon or orange)
- 1 teaspoon vanilla extract

- 1 ½ – 2 cups blueberries, fresh or frozen
- Optional garnish
- A few extra blueberries
- Sprinkle of cane sugar

PREPARATION

Preheat the furnace to 350°F.

Mix the wet ingredients: pour in a 2 cup measuring cup the milk, sugar, oil and vanilla and swirl to combine a few times to help soften the large sugar grains.

Mix the dry ingredients together: In a large mixing bowl, mix the flour, baking powder and salt together.

Combine wet & dry: pour the wet mixture into the dry mixture and blend until just mixed. It seems that overmixing the batter makes the muffins less tender. Only don't overmix.

Add the blueberries: With the fresh or frozen ones, toss the blueberries and fold them gently into the batter.

Scoop: Fill with batter any void lined with muffins. Using a 1/4 measuring cup or a large ice cream scooper to scoop up the batter for consistency and pour into the muffin holes to fill the muffin tray.

Topping: Add some strategic blueberries on top of the option and sprinkle on top with some pure cane sugar or raw sugar. The sugar will give a nice crunch to the tops!

Bake: In the oven, put the mixture and cook for 30 minutes. Enable a few minutes to cool and drink at room temperature or warmer.

Creates 12 muffins

STORING:

Counter & Fridge: Once fully cooled, with a paper towel underneath, store the muffins in a jar on the counter for up to 3 to 4 days. The paper towels will soak up moisture and stop them from becoming too moist, losing their delicious crunchy top. They are also fine, loosely covered, for 1-2 days. Or store it in the refrigerator for up to a week.

Freezer: Once fully cooled, seal the muffins individually and place them in a freezer-safe container or baggie for up to 2 months. Leave to thaw until ready for feeding at room temperature.

VEGAN LOX SANDWICH

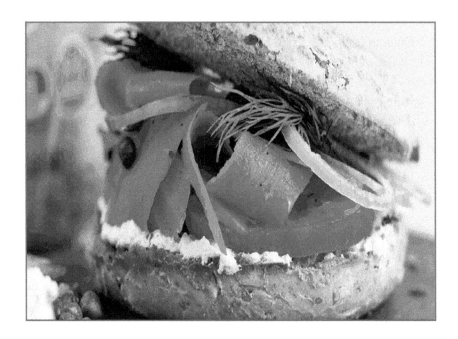

SERVINGS: 2

INGREDIENTS

- Vegan Lox
- 3 large carrots, washed
- 1 tablespoon olive oil
- 1 cup water
- 1 tablespoon soy sauce
- 2 teaspoons vegan Worcestershire sauce
- 1 teaspoon liquid smoke
- 2 nori sheets, broken into bits
- Bagel Sandwich
- 2 Alvarado St. Bakery Sprouted Wheat Bagels
- 1 roma tomato, sliced

- 1/2 red onion, thinly sliced
- vegan cream cheese
- fresh dill
- capers
- salt and pepper

PREPARATION

Preheat the oven to 400. Brush the carrots with the aid of olive oil and arrange them on a baking sheet. Bake for 30 minutes until it is tender and fragrant. Meanwhile, whisk together the remaining ingredients of the lox and transfer to a shallow dish.

Using a vegetable peeler, cut the carrots into thin strips. In the marinade, put the carrots, making sure they are fully submerged. Cover and refrigerate for at least 30 minutes. It is also possible the night before to do this.

To make the bagel sandwiches, break the bagels in half and toast lightly. Spread out all the layers of cream cheese and top with tomatoes, carrot lox, onions, fresh dill, and capers.

Serve instantly.

GREEN SPELLED RISOTTO WITH FRIED KING OYSTER MUSHROOMS AND RADICCHIO

SERVINGS 2

INGREDIENTS

- 175 g green spelled
- 1 onion
- 1 toe garlic
- 4 tbsp rapeseed oil with butter flavor
- ½ teaspoon salt
- 1 sprig of thyme

- 750 ml vegetable stock
- 75 g king oyster mushrooms
- ½ tsp smoked salt
- 40 g vegan parmesan
- 80 g radicchio
- ½ teaspoon maple syrup
- 10 g chives
- ½ teaspoon black pepper coarsely ground

PREPARATION

Grind spelled green with the Kitchen Aid grinder attachment at the coarsest setting.

Dice the onion finely, peel and press on the garlic. In a hot saucepan, add 2 tablespoons of oil, sauté the onion and garlic for 2 minutes over medium heat and season with salt. Attach the crushed spelled green and the thyme sprig, fry over high heat for another minute, then deglaze with 250 ml of vegetable stock and bring it to a boil.

Cook the green spelled risotto for 25 minutes over low to medium heat, progressively adding the remaining vegetable stock as soon as the pan has absorbed almost all of the liquid.

Meanwhile, cut the king oyster mushrooms into 1/2 cm thick slices, place the remaining oil in a hot pan and fry the mushrooms on each side for around 4-5 minutes over medium to high heat until golden brown. Season, eventually, with smoked salt.

5 minutes before the end of cooking time, fold the vegan Parmesan under the risotto.

Take the mushrooms out of the pan, pluck the radicchio approximately into bite-sized pieces and stir-fry on high heat for 1 minute in the still hot pan and season with maple syrup.

Cover the raddichio, mushrooms and freshly chopped chives with the risotto and season with pepper.

SUGGESTIONS

The choice of milling whole grain on site is also provided by some organic markets. It's better if you don't have your own flour mill to ask the workers about the coarsest environment.

PUMPKIN HASH BROWNS WITH CASHEW MISO DIP

SERVINGS 4

INGREDIENTS

- For the pumpkin hash browns
- 1 kg pumpkin z. B. Hokkaido, butternut or nutmeg
- 2 teaspoons of salt
- 100 g whole wheat flour or whole spelled flour
- 1 ½ tbsp potato starch
- ½ teaspoon of allspice
- 4 tbsp olive oil

- For the onions
- 1 red onion
- ¾ teaspoon salt
- 2 tbsp apple cider vinegar
- For the cashew miso dip
- 125 g cashew nuts
- 1 teaspoon light miso paste
- Squeezed out ½ lemon juice
- ¼ teaspoon salt
- ½ teaspoon garlic powder
- Furthermore
- 15 g parsley

PREPARATION

Grate the pumpkin roughly with the food processor or kitchen grater. In a sufficiently large tub, mix with salt, massage gently with your hands and leave to steep for 10 minutes.

Meanwhile, dice the onion finely, mix it with salt and vinegar and set it aside.

In a mixer or high-speed blender, finely purée the cashew nuts with miso, lemon juice, salt, garlic powder and 125 ml of water.

Drain the grated pumpkin with your hands and squeeze the excess liquid out well. Put the wholemeal flour and potato flour back in the cup, season with allspice, and knead briefly.

In a hot pan, add the olive oil, shape 12 hash browns and fry on each side for 4-5 minutes, one after the other, until golden brown.

Top and serve hot with cashew miso dip, onions and finely chopped parsley.

SUGGESTIONS

Of course, the pumpkin rösti tastes best out of the pan, fresh and crispy. Let the hash browns drain briefly on kitchen paper if you have to feed more hungry mouths, and then keep them warm in the oven at 120 ° C before serving.

The ready-mixed dough can be kept in the fridge, tightly closed. And for up to five days, too. In between, nothing stands in the way of a fast rösti.

QUICK KALE PAN WITH WHITE BEANS & SUNDRIED TOMATOES

SERVINGS 2

INGREDIENTS

- 20 g dried tomatoes
- 1 onion
- 200 g kale
- 3 cloves of garlic
- 2 tbsp olive oil
- 1 teaspoon salt
- 350 g cooked white beans

- ½ teaspoon black pepper
- ½ tsp chilli flakes
- For the tahini sauce
- 50 g tahini
- 50 ml of soaking water for the tomatoes
- Squeezed out 1/2 lemon juice
- Salt if necessary
- For the millet
- 120 g millet
- ¾ teaspoon salt

PREPARATION

Over the sun-dried tomatoes, add 100 ml of boiling water and let it steep for 10 minutes.

In 350 ml of water, bring the millet to a boil, boil for 5 minutes, season with salt, remove from the stove and leave to swell with the lid closed for 10 minutes.

Meanwhile, cut the onions into fine strips, cut the kale stalks into pieces that are around 2 cm long, and chop the greens roughly. Pick up the soaking water. Drain the tomatoes. Thinly slice the garlic and cut the tomatoes into fine strips.

Put the oil in a hot pan or saucepan and sauté the onions for 2 minutes over medium heat. Add the tomatoes and garlic, season with 1/2 teaspoon of salt and fry for another 2 minutes.

Fold in the kale gradually, let it collapse and stew for 5-7 minutes.

Stir the tahini with half the tomato water for the sauce, and the lemon juice with a whisk until smooth.

Attach the beans to the kale, add the remaining soaking water, season with the chili and pepper, bring to a boil and serve on top of the millet.

VEGAN TARTE FLAMBÉE

SERVINGS 4

INGREDIENTS

- For the tarte flambée batter
- 105 g wheat flour type 405
- 0.7 g dry yeast
- 2.5 g of salt
- 1.5 g of sugar
- 5 g olive oil
- 64 g of water
- For covering
- 50 g Creme VEGA

- 25 g unsweetened soy yogurt
- ¼ teaspoon salt
- 1 pinch of nutmeg
- ½ red onion
- 60 g vegan seitan bacon or smoked tofu
- ½ teaspoon olive oil
- ¼ teaspoon black pepper
- 1 pinch of salt
- 7 g flat leaf parsley

PREPARATION

Mix the rice, yeast, sugar and salt approximately together for the dough. To shape a smooth, even dough, add olive oil and water and knead for 10 minutes using your hands or a food processor. Shape it into a round shape, put it back in the tub, cover it and let it stand in a warm spot. If you are cooking more than one flambée tart, split the dough into individual parts at this stage and let it rise.

Preheat the top / bottom heat of the oven to 260 ° C with a pizza stone or baking sheet.

Dr. Blend Creme VEGA with soy yogurt for topping and season with salt and nutmeg. Until occupied, set aside.

Halve the onion and cut into thin strips, cut into 5 mm cubes or 5 mm thick strips of seitan 'bacon' or smoked tofu.

Moisten one dough piece lightly with oil and roll it out rather thinly on the work surface or on baking paper to a diameter of around 30 cm.

Brush with Creme VEGA, cover with strips of onion, seitan or tofu and drizzle with some oil. Bake for 5-7 minutes and then serve with salt and parsley topping.

SUGGESTIONS

Any wheat and spelled flour that is not too coarsely ground works basically. Fine flour from wheat, e.g. B. It is easier to grind Tipo 00 pizza flour.

VEGAN CREAM OF MUSHROOM SOUP

INGREDIENTS

- 1 onion
- 1 toe garlic
- 500 g mushrooms
- 3 tbsp rapeseed oil with butter flavor
- 2 sprigs of thyme leaves plucked
- ¾ teaspoon salt
- 1 ½ tbsp wheat flour type 405 or spelled flour type 630
- 250 ml vegan white wine
- 750 ml vegetable stock

- 4 tbsp vegan crème fraîche
- ½ teaspoon ground black pepper
- Finely dice the onion and garlic, cut the mushrooms into slices.
- Set aside 12 large, beautiful slices for the topping.

PREPARATION

In a hot saucepan, place 1 tablespoon of oil, simmer the onion, garlic, thyme and remaining mushrooms over medium to high heat, stirring regularly until the mushrooms have drained and most of the water has evaporated. It takes approximately seven minutes. Take the mushrooms out of the jar, then set them aside.

Add 1 tablespoon of oil and flour and stir-fry for 1 minute until the flour is lightly browned. Place the pot back on the burner. Deglaze with white wine and stir with a whisk in 3 tablespoons of vegan crème fraîche. Pour the vegetable stock, bring to a boil, and simmer for 15 minutes. Add the mushroom and onion vegetables.

Pour the remaining oil into a hot pan and fry the mushrooms over medium to high heat for approximately 3-5 minutes on each side.

Finely purée the broth, top with the remaining crème fraîche, the fresh thyme and pepper, the sauteed mushrooms and serve with bread.

VEGAN WHOLEMEAL WAFFLES WITH KIWI QUARK

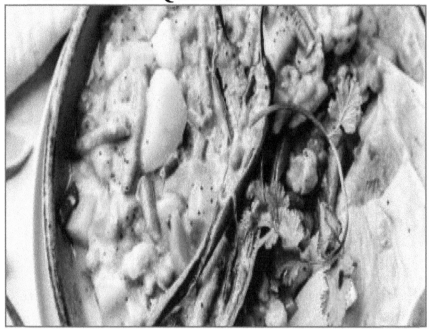

SERVINGS 2 FOR 6 WAFFLES

INGREDIENTS

- For the wholemeal waffles
- 250 g whole spelled flour or whole wheat flour
- 1 ½ tbsp psyllium husks
- 2 teaspoons of baking powder
- 1 pinch of salt
- 475 ml of oat milk or another type of vegetable milk
- 2 tbsp hazelnut oil or rapeseed oil or olive oil + about 1 tbsp for oiling the waffle iron
- 3 drops of vanilla extract optional

- 2 teaspoons maple syrup
- For the kiwi quark
- 2 kiwis z. B. Zespri Green Kiwi
- 200 g vegan quark or vegan skyr
- Furthermore
- 20 g roasted pumpkin seeds
- 20 g roasted sunflower seeds
- Maple syrup optional

PREPARATION

Blend the flour, psyllium husks, baking powder and salt together for the waffles. Add oat milk, oil, vanilla extract and maple syrup and mix to make a smooth, not too runny batter that runs out of the spoon and is firm. Add a tablespoon of water if necessary.

Waffles for Vegan

Let it soak when preheating the waffle iron for 5 minutes.

Break the kiwifruit into small pieces for the kiwi quark, and stir it into the vegan quark. As a topping, save a few bits.

Oil the waffle iron lightly, add the batter - approximately 3 heaping tablespoons per waffle, depending on the shape size - and bake for 4-8 minutes, depending on the waffle iron output.

Serve warm waffles topped with kiwi quark, maple syrup, and roasted seeds.

CREAMY VEGAN PUMPKIN NOODLE BAKE

SERVINGS 4

INGREDIENTS

- 1 onion
- 2 tbsp olive oil
- 2 cloves garlic
- 450 g pumpkin z. B. Butternut
- ¾ teaspoon thyme leaves plucked
- ½ tsp chilli flakes
- 1 teaspoon salt
- For the sauce
- 150 ml almond milk or oat milk or soy milk

- 75 g soy yogurt
- 2 EL Hefeflocken
- 125 ml white wine
- ¾ teaspoon salt
- ½ teaspoon black pepper
- 3 tbsp vegan grated cheese
- Furthermore
- 300 g conchiglie
- 40 g vegan grated cheese
- 15 g parsley

PREPARATION

For 3 minutes, cut the onion into fine strips, pour the oil into a hot, oven-safe saucepan and caramelize the strips of onion over low to medium heat.

Preheat the oven to a top / bottom heat of 180 ° C.

Chop the garlic thinly and cut the pumpkin into cubes about 2 cm long. To the saucepan with thyme and chilli flakes, add the garlic and pumpkin, season with salt and stew for another 5 minutes. Stirring on occasion.

Meanwhile, combine the INGREDIENTS with 350 ml of water for the sauce.

Fold the conchiglie under the vegetables of the pumpkin, deglaze with the sauce, bring to a boil and cook in the oven for 20 minutes with the lid. Then remove the lid, stir well, sprinkle with grated vegan cheese and bake without the lid for 10 minutes. Cover with parsley that is finely chopped.

SUGGESTIONS

The white wine can be supplemented with the most acidic grape juice and a little apple cider vinegar or lemon juice.

Our vegan mozzarella is perfect for gratinating instead of the vegan grated cheese, too.

SIMPLE VEGETABLE RICE FROM THE OVEN

SERVINGS 4

INGREDIENTS

- 1 onion
- 2 cloves of garlic
- 3 tbsp olive oil
- 175 g zucchini
- 150 g green peppers
- 75 g red pepper
- 240 g Bonduelle À LA REIS Red Lentils & Carrots

- 1 ½ tsp oregano gerebelt
- 1 teaspoon paprika powder
- 1 teaspoon salt
- ½ teaspoon black pepper coarsely ground
- ½ teaspoon lemon zest
- 650 ml vegetable broth
- 150 g cherry tomatoes
- For the lemon yogurt
- 4 tbsp soy yogurt
- 3 tbsp lemon juice
- ½ teaspoon salt
- Furthermore
- 15 g parsley

PREPARATION

Preheat the oven to a top / bottom heat of 180 ° C.

Dice the onion and slice the garlic finely. Put the olive oil in an ovenproof saucepan or deep frying pan and sauté the onion and garlic over low to medium heat for 3 minutes, stirring frequently.

Break the zucchini and peppers into cubes measuring 2 cm. Together with Bonduelle À LA REIS, add red lentils & carrots to the pan, fry for another 2 minutes over high heat, season with oregano, paprika powder, salt, pepper and lemon zest, deglaze with vegetable stock and bring to a boil for a short time.

Spread the cherry tomatoes on the vegetable rice, preferably in a panicle, and then cook in the oven for 30 minutes on the middle rack. For the last 5 minutes, turn to top heat.

Mix the soy yoghurt with the lemon juice for the lemon yoghurt and season with salt.

erve the vegetable rice topped with the finely chopped parsley and lemon yogurt.

VEGAN FRIED RICE WITH TOFU EGG

SERVINGS 4

INGREDIENTS

1. For the rice
2. 160 g jasmine rice is equivalent to about 325 g cooled rice
3. For the tofu egg
4. 100 g tofu
5. 1 EL neutral frying oil or peanut oil
6. 1 ½ tbsp soy yogurt

7. ¼ tsp turmeric powder
8. ¼ tsp kala namak
9. Furthermore
10. 1 spring onion
11. 50 g carrot
12. 50 g green beans
13. 3 cloves of garlic
14. 2 EL neutral frying oil or peanut oil
15. 50 g peas
16. 50 g corn
17. ¾ teaspoon salt
18. ½ teaspoon white pepper
19. 2 tbsp soy sauce
20. 1 tsp dark soy sauce optional
21. 1 teaspoon sesame oil optional

PREPARATION

Because of the RICE

Cook jasmine rice in a rice cooker or in a saucepan with 1.2 times the amount of water, as mentioned here. Spread on a baking sheet or large plate and leave to cool, as mentioned in the document, in the refrigerator.

FOR TOFU 'EGG'

Split into thin slices of tofu. On high heat, preheat the wok, add the oil, toss well over the bottom and sides, and brown the tofu for 5 minutes over low to medium heat, stirring frequently. Stir in turmeric and soy yogurt, cook for 3 minutes, season with Kala Namak, remove from the wok and set aside.

Because of the Fried Rice

Cut the white portion of the carrot of the spring onion, carrot and green beans into bits or cubes of pea size. Cut the greens of the spring onion into fine rings and set aside for the garnish, then chop the garlic finely.

Wipe the wok thoroughly, heat up again, add the remaining oil, toss well over the base and sides and cook the onion, carrot and beans for 2 minutes over high heat.

Add the garlic, peas and corn, fry for another 2 minutes, add the rice and add the salt and pepper to taste. Do not press the rice too hard on the base of the wok with the spatula and then loosen it up afterward. Stir the pan until it is al dente with the vegetables and the rice turns a light golden yellow color.

Heat briefly and serve hot with, for example, cucumber slices and chili oil, deglaze with light and dark soy sauce and sesame oil, blend evenly, add in the tofu 'egg' and chopped spring onion greens.

KOHLRABI VEGETABLE

SERVINGS 4

INGREDIENTS

- 1 kg of kohlrabi
- 500 g carrots
- 35 g parsley
- 10 g lovage optional
- 2 tbsp rapeseed oil with butter flavor
- 4 tbsp wheat flour type 405
- 200 ml of oat milk
- 1 ½ tsp salt
- 1 EL Hefeflocken

- 1 pinch of nutmeg
- 1 teaspoon black pepper

PREPARATION

Slice the kohlrabi and carrots into 2 cm cubes and cook until al dente for 3 minutes in a saucepan with boiling salted water.

Drain, gather 300 ml of boiling water from the vegetables and set aside.

The parsley and lovage are separately finely chopped.

Put the oil in a hot saucepan, add the flour gradually over medium heat while stirring so that the oil quickly still absorbs the flour and does not form lumps.

Sweat until the paste is lightly browned, for 1-2 minutes while stirring.

Mix the cooking water and oat milk reserved for vegetables and stir gradually with a whisk into the roux. Season with salt to taste.

Add the vegetables, flakes of yeast, nutmeg, lovage and half the parsley, bring to a boil and simmer for 15 minutes over low heat with the lid closed.

The remaining fresh parsley and freshly ground black pepper are eaten topped with potatoes or boiled potatoes.

SUGGESTIONS

For sauces and stews, which is not called "Maggi herb" for nothing, we also like to use lovage. The herb gives every dish a lot of flavor! Getting into the supermarket isn't that easy, but on the kitchen window sill, a potty like this from the nursery is also perfect.

VEGAN BEEF AND BROCCOLI

SERVINGS 4

INGREDIENTS

- 7 g grated ginger
- 1 toe garlic rubbed
- 1 tbsp soy sauce
- 1 tbsp cornstarch
- 300 g seitan beef
- 1 onion
- 300 g broccoli
- 2 tbsp peanut oil
- For the sauce

- 4 tbsp soy sauce
- 1 tbsp mirin optional
- 1 tbsp sesame oil
- 1 TL cane sugar
- 1 toe garlic rubbed
- Furthermore
- 4 tbsp toasted sesame seeds

PREPARATION

Stir together the grated ginger and garlic with soy sauce and cornstarch for the marinade. Break the seitan into thin strips, mix well and apply to the marinade.

Cut the onion into strips, split the broccoli into florets and, if necessary, cut them into bite-sized pieces. Mix all the INGREDIENTS with 75 ml of water and set aside for the sauce.

Put in a hot wok or pan about 100 ml of water, steam broccoli and lid on for 1 1/2-2 minutes over high heat, until most of the water has evaporated. Drain, rinse and drain well under cold water.

Apply the peanut oil and stir-fry the seitan and onion over high heat for 3 minutes until both are lightly caramelized. Place the wok back on the burner.

Attach the broccoli, then fry for 3 more minutes. Then deglaze with the sauce, bring to the boil while stirring and simmer until the sauce is slightly thick for around 2 minutes.

Cover with toasted seeds of sesame and serve with noodles of jasmine rice, rice or wheat.

SUGGESTIONS

Instead of seitan, tofu or soy medallions can also be used. Cut the tofu into slices about 5 mm thick, soak the soy medallions before further processing according to the product instructions and squeeze them well before marinating.

GREEN PAELLA WITH BEANS, PEAS & SNOW PEAS

SERVINGS 4

INGREDIENTS

- 2 shallots
- 2 cloves of garlic
- 2 tbsp olive oil
- 1 teaspoon salt
- ½ teaspoon coriander seeds ground
- 200 g green beans
- 75 g celery sticks

- 240 g Bonduelle À LA REIS Peas & Zucchini
- 300 ml white wine
- 400 ml vegetable broth
- 175 g artichoke hearts in brine
- 100 g sugar snap peas
- 100 g peas
- Furthermore
- 1 green chilli
- 1 lime
- 10 g coriander

PREPARATION

Chop the shallots and garlic finely. Place the olive oil in a hot pan and sauté the onion and garlic for 3 minutes over low to medium heat, stirring frequently. Connect the seeds of salt and coriander and fry for a further 2 minutes.

Halve the beans, cut the celery into 2 cm bits, add them to the pan and fry over high heat for 4 minutes.

Stir in Bonduelle À LA REIS peas & zucchini, add wine and vegetable stock to deglaze and cook for 20 minutes over low heat. Rarely stir. Add 50 ml of water if required.

Drain the artichokes, half or quarter depending on the scale, and at an angle, halve the snow peas. Fold the peas into the rice 5 minutes before the cooking time ends, and switch the heat to low.

Serve with thinly sliced chili, lime wedges and plucked coriander leaves served with green paella.

SUGGESTIONS

Depending on the form of rice, whether you use round grain or paella rice, you have to increase the cooking time by around 5-10 minutes.

A rice pan is also a great recipe for recycling leftovers, of course (even if I will now get even more anger from the purists with this statement). Aren't there any snap peas in the fridge for you? Then take the remaining slice of zucchini, half the green bell pepper or the plucked kale or black cabbage leaves that are still in the vegetable compartment.

FILLED ZUCCHINI BOATS WITH VEGAN MINCED MEAT

SERVINGS 4 FOR 4 ZUCCHINI BOATS

INGREDIENTS

- 2 zucchini approx. 600 g
- 1 olive oil z. B. from EDEKA
- 1 teaspoon salt
- 275 g vegan minced meat e.g. B. "No Meat. Just Hack." from EDEKA
- 1 onion
- 2 cloves garlic

- 1 teaspoon fennel seeds
- 1 teaspoon coriander seeds
- 1 tbsp tomato paste z. B. from EDEKA
- 1 teaspoon thyme
- ½ tsp chilli flakes
- ¼ tsp allspice
- ½ teaspoon black pepper coarsely ground
- 30 g olives
- 50 g vegan grated cheese
- Furthermore
- 10 g basil
- 10 g parsley

PREPARATION

Preheat the oven to a top / bottom heat of 200 ° C.

Halve the zucchini and use a spoon to scrape out the seeds.

Rub the zucchini halves with olive oil all over and season with 1/2 teaspoon salt and pre-cook for 10 minutes on the middle rack on a baking sheet lined with baking paper.

The Filling for the Filling

Grate the onion with a grater of vegetables (collect the onion juice), grate the garlic finely, mortar the seeds of the fennel and coriander.

Along with tomato paste, thyme, chilli flakes and allspice, add to the vegan minced meat. Mix well and apply the pepper and the remaining salt to season.

In the precooked zucchini boats, pour the mince filling and press down well. Top with pitted and sliced olives and vegan cheese, and cook for 20-25 minutes on the middle rack.

Top with finely chopped herbs and serve with, for instance, rice or a broad mixed salad.

SUGGESTIONS

Don't salt the vegan minced meat mixture too much if pickled olives are used.

BRAISED SWISS CHARD ON TAHINI LEMON YOGURT

SERVINGS 4

INGREDIENTS

- For the chard
- 1 onion
- 8 cloves of garlic
- 1 yellow chilli
- 750 g Swiss chard
- 6 rapeseed oil and butter flavor or olive oil
- 1 ½ tsp salt
- 1 tbsp lemon juice
- ½ teaspoon black pepper
- For the tahini yogurt
- 40 g tahini
- 80 g soy yogurt or another vegetable yogurt alternative
- 1 freshly squeezed lemon
- ½ teaspoon salt
- Furthermore
- 30 g basil

PREPARATION

Finely chop the onion, garlic and chili for the vegetables. Break the chard into bits that are bite-sized.

Put the oil in a hot saucepan and sauté the onion, garlic and chili over medium heat for 3 minutes. Stirring on occasion. Connect the stalks of chard and fry for a further 2 minutes.

Use salt to season, add the leaves and stir well. Simmer with the lid closed for 10 minutes over low to medium sun. Stirring on occasion.

Meanwhile, combine the tahini, vegetable yogurt, 100 ml of water and salt with the lemon juice, and set aside.

Using lemon juice to season the chard and serve on top of tahini-lemon yogurt. Cover with new basil and black pepper and serve immediately.

VEGAN YELLOW THAI CURRY

FOR 4 SERVINGS

INGREDIENTS

- For the curry paste (for approx. 6 tbsp)
- 4 shallots
- 4 cloves of garlic
- 1 stick of lemongrass
- 1 red Thai chili
- 1 TL Galgantpulver or 10 g of fresh galangal
- 15 g fresh turmeric root
- 15 g coriander

- 2 tbsp curry powder
- 4 tbsp soy sauce
- 2 EL panel ethyl
- 2 TL light miso paste
- For the curry
- 2 onions
- 225 g carrot
- 300 g potato
- 2 tbsp peanut oil
- 1-2 pkg LikeMeat Like Chicken
- 3 tbsp curry paste
- 400 ml coconut milk
- 15 g coriander

PREPARATION

For the Paste of Curry

The dry outer leaves are stripped from the lemongrass, the stalk and the tip are cut off, and the rest are loosely cut into rings. Peel and roughly chop the turmeric along with the shallots, garlic, chili and cilantro.

In a large mortar or in a food processor, purée all the ingredients except the miso paste into a fine paste. Stir in the miso paste then.

The curry paste in the refrigerator can be kept tightly closed for up to 14 days.

For the curry, for the

Break the onions, carrots and potatoes into bits that are bite-sized.

In a hot saucepan, put the oil, sear the Like Chicken for 2 minutes over medium to high heat, stirring frequently, then remove from the saucepan and set aside.

To the saucepan, apply the curry paste and 3 tablespoons of coconut milk and stir-fry for 2 minutes over medium to high heat. Add the vegetables, deglaze with the remaining 200 ml of coconut milk and water, bring to a boil and simmer for 15 minutes over low to medium heat with the lid on. Return the chicken to the pot and let it steep for another 5 minutes.

Using coriander greens to top and serve with jasmine rice.

VEGAN KIMCHI SPAETZLE

INGREDIENTS

For the spaetzle

- 160 g wheat flour type 405 or spaetzle flour or wheat steam
- 40 g durum wheat semolina
- 1 teaspoon salt
- 1 teaspoon kala namak
- 1 TL Gochugaru
- 2 teaspoons of olive oil
- 150 ml of oat milk
- 50 ml of water

- Furthermore
- ½ onion
- ½ tbsp olive oil
- 175 g kimchi
- 1 tbsp gochujang
- 75 g vegan grated cheese
- 10 g chives

PREPARATION

FOR THE SPAETZLE

Mix loosely with rice, semolina, salt, Kala Namak and Gochugaru. Add oil, oat milk, and water and whisk vigorously to form a smooth, viscous dough.

Press into boiling water with a spaetzle maker or a spaetzle press, stir and remove from the water with a skimmer as soon as the spaetzle is floating on the surface. Let's drain them briefly.

KIMCHI SPAETZLE FOR

Split into strips with the onion. In a hot pan, put the oil, fry the onion and spaetzle while stirring for 2 minutes.

Chop the kimchi roughly, add the gochujang to the pan, and fry for a further 3 minutes. Stir in vegan cheese, let it briefly melt and serve with chives on top.

VEGAN BEER FONDUE WITH PUMPKIN

FOR 1 LITER

INGREDIENTS

- 4 tbsp rapeseed oil with butter flavor
- 300 g smoked tofu z. B. from EDEKA Bio naturally vegan
- 350 g Hokkaido pumpkin corresponds to approx. 300 g peeled
- 75 g potato
- 1 ½ tsp salt

- 50 g cashew nuts z. B. from EDEKA Bio
- 3 cloves of garlic
- 400 ml of beer sweet and not too tart - e.g. B. a light, cellar or full beer
- 250 ml oat milk e.g. B. from EDEKA Bio naturally vegan
- 1 teaspoon mustard
- 1 EL light miso paste
- 2 tbsp white wine vinegar
- 5 EL Hefeflocken
- 3 tbsp tapioca starch

PREPARATION

Slice the smoked tofu into 2 cm cubes then use kitchen paper to pat it dry.

Put the oil in a hot saucepan and fry the smoked tofu for 7-10 minutes over medium heat until it is golden brown. Peel the pumpkin, meanwhile, and loosely dice it along with the potato. Push on the garlic and chop roughly.

Take the cubes of tofu from the pot, enabling the oil to drain well. For serving, set the tofu aside.

To the saucepan, add the pumpkin and potato, season with 1 teaspoon of salt and cook for 2 minutes over medium to high heat. Attach the cashew nuts and garlic and fry for 2 more minutes.

Deglaze with beer and oat milk, season with mustard and simmer for 20 minutes until the vegetables are tender, with the lid closed. Take it off the stove then and let it cool down. Meanwhile, have the side dishes ready.

In a high-speed blender or with a hand mixer, purée the contents of the pot along with the miso paste, vinegar, yeast flakes and starch. The consistency should be close to that of a pumpkin soup that is not too liquid, season to taste with the remaining salt and, if appropriate, dilute with oat milk or water.

Bring it back to the saucepan and bring it back to the boil when stirring. Keep stirring until slightly tough and threads are pulled by the vegan cheese fondue.

In the fondue pot, pour hot and serve with all of the dip side dishes of your choosing.

SUGGESTIONS

Our absolute side dish favourites at a glance here again:

Tofu Smoked

Getting mixed pickles

Hearts of Artichoke

Onions of Silver

Slices of beetroot

Olives in the Green

Various vegetables such as potatoes, broccoli, carrots etc. are cooked and blanched.

SALSIFY VEGETABLES WITH ROASTED PINE NUTS

FOR 4 SERVINGS

INGREDIENTS

- 500 g black salsify
- 3 tbsp pine nuts z. B. from the pine nut campaign
- 1 shallot
- 3 tbsp olive oil
- 2 cloves garlic
- ½ tsp smoked salt
- ½ teaspoon black pepper ground

- 2 tbsp soy sauce
- 20 g parsley
- 1 teaspoon cornstarch

PREPARATION

1 Lemon Juice Squeezed Out

Peel the black salsify (see tip), cut into slices about 1 cm thick diagonally. Blanch for 8 minutes in salted boiling water, then drain and drain well.

For 4 minutes, roast the pine nuts in a pan without oil, stirring frequently. Remove it from the pan, then set it aside.

Dice the shallot finely, add the oil to the pan, fry the black salsify and shallot for 10 minutes over a medium to high heat, stirring occasionally. Season with smoked salt and pepper and deglaze with the soy sauce, cut the garlic into fine slices, fold into the salsify.

Chop the parsley finely and set aside about 3 teaspoons. Stir the cornstarch in 150 ml of cold water, add it to the pan, bring it to a boil for a moment, then let it steep over low heat for 2 minutes. Just before eating, whisk in the lemon juice. Serve the roasted pine nuts and the remaining parsley on top.

SUGGESTIONS

Salsify is best washed off and peeled with rubber gloves under running water, so the juice can turn black on your hands. Before drying, peeled salsify can then be preserved in vinegar water. For 1 liter of water, add about 2 tablespoons of white vinegar.

Blanched salsify - again in vinegar water - can be preserved for 1-2 days or frozen in the refrigerator.

BÁNH TRÁNG TRÔN - VIETNAMESE RICE PAPER SALAD

FOR 2 SERVINGS

INGREDIENTS

For the fried shallots

- 75 g shallots
- 50 ml of sunflower oil
- 1/2 teaspoon salt
- For the soy jerky
- 50 g soy medallions
- 2 tbsp soy sauce
- 1 tbsp dark soy sauce
- 1 teaspoon pepper flakes

- 1/4 teaspoon black pepper
- For the dressing
- 1 tbsp tamarind paste
- 3 tbsp soy sauce
- 2 teaspoons of sugar
- Squeezed out 1 lime juice
- 3 tbsp water
- Furthermore
- 350 g kohlrabi
- 12 sheets of rice paper approx. 120 g
- 40 g roasted peanuts
- 40 g Vietnamese coriander leaves plucked

PREPARATION

Crop the shallots into fine rings for the fried shallots. Pour oil into a small saucepan and heat until around a wooden spoon held in the saucepan, bubbles emerge. Fry the shallots for 15-20 minutes over medium heat until they are golden brown. Remove from the oil, drain on kitchen paper and apply salt to the seasoning.

Meanwhile, soak the soy medallions for 10 minutes in plenty of warm water. Then pour out, squeeze well and cut into 5 mm short strips.

Put 1 tbsp of shallot oil in a hot pan and fry soy strips for 5 minutes over medium to high heat until crispy. Stir occasionally. Season with chili flakes and pepper, stir well, turn off the heat and set aside until eaten. Deglaze with soy sauce.

Mix all the ingredients together with 1 tbsp of shallot oil to make the dressing.

Slice the kohlrabi into thin mandolin strips, cut the rice paper into 3 x 5 cm pieces, chop the peanuts roughly, and pluck the coriander leaves.

Mix bits of rice paper into the remaining ingredients gradually to serve, mix with the dressing and serve immediately.

SUGGESTIONS

They should cook the fried shallots in advance. They can be kept airtight and stored for up to 7 days in a cool spot. When they are baked in the oven at about 120 ° C for 10 minutes, they taste best, so they will become crispy again even after a longer storage time.

If it is tightly closed and also stored in a cool and dry spot, the remaining shallot oil is kept for at least a month.

CONCLUSION

Obesity is one of the greatest civilization problems of our time. We present the advantages of a vegan diet and support you with important tips.

So folks, there are really many reasons to be vegan. You just have to read the newspaper or watch the news regularly, then you don't really need to think twice: Be it the regularly recurring food scandals, catastrophic conditions in factory farming, reports on advancing climate change. So it's no wonder that every day more and more people are obviously opting for a vegan diet.

Animal welfare is undoubtedly the number one motivation for this not entirely insignificant life decision. In the past, many people had concerns about embarking on a vegan lifestyle for health reasons - keyword "malnutrition" - but recently we have been experiencing exactly the opposite trend. In the meantime, we are increasingly being asked for shopping tips and vegan recipes, especially from our non-vegan circle of friends. The reason: Obviously, you can lose weight quite easily with a vegan diet without having to forego enjoyment.

Eat yourself slim

No question about it, when it comes to losing weight, of course, a certain ideal of beauty also plays a role for one or the other. But most of the people we talked to are primarily concerned with feeling good - because every pound less on the ribs is a relief in the truest sense of the word. However, there is an increasingly larger group that is dedicated to the topic for health reasons. In the meantime, word has got around that a vegan diet can alleviate or even prevent numerous diseases. Above all, all diseases related to excess fat and obesity. Starting with high blood pressure, which is known to lead to heart attacks and strokes, metabolic diseases to cancer.

A particularly large group for whom a vegan diet is becoming increasingly interesting are all those who are at risk of developing diabetes.

Vegan diet reduces the risk of diabetes

Around 250 million people worldwide suffer from diabetes mellitus. In Germany, around one in ten is now affected. Roughly speaking, a distinction is made between 2 types of the disease, type 1 diabetes mellitus and type 2. Type 1 diabetes mellitus is an autoimmune disease, the development of which is independent of diet.

The far greater proportion, however, suffer from type 2 - an estimated 80–90% of diabetics. This is a typical affluence disease associated with poor nutrition, obesity and lack of exercise. This results in insulin resistance, which means that insulin cannot work adequately on target tissues such as the skeletal muscles. The reason: too much fatty acid in the blood, which leads to an increased concentration of glucose, which in turn leads to the production of so much insulin, which in the long term ultimately leads to the exhaustion of insulin and even failure of insulin formation.

A very recent study found that a "vegan diet improves insulin resistance in obese people". Which in normal language does not mean that people who are vegetarian-vegan have a much lower risk of developing type 2 diabetes mellitus. This is due to the fact that this metabolic disease is usually triggered by a high-fat diet - i.e. too much meat consumption.

A vegan diet that completely dispenses with animal products, on the other hand, does two things: On the one hand, the significant reduction in the fat content in the food also reduces fat deposits in the liver. And since fatty liver plays a crucial role in the development of insulin resistance, a source of danger is reduced. On the other hand, the vegan diet improves the glucose metabolism. Because almost all types of fruit and vegetables have a low glycemic index. This can have a positive effect on the carbohydrate metabolism. As a result, carbohydrates are metabolized more quickly and literally do not set in.

The result: loss of adipose tissue, weight and thus a lower risk of diabetes.

So the best cure for diabetes is to lose weight. And that's especially easy with a vegan diet. But what should you watch out for?

Vegan does not automatically mean losing weight

We'll have to pull a tooth right away. Eating vegan doesn't mean that you automatically lose weight. You can also get fat as a vegan. But then you are definitely doing something wrong. Whether you gain or lose weight is not decided by the composition of the food, but by its amount: If you eat more calories than you burn, you will also gain weight. If there are fewer calories, then the pounds drop.

But it is also a fact that people who live vegan have a significantly lower body mass index (BMI) compared to meat eaters , i.e. they are usually slimmer. Why? First, because we eat less unhealthy meat or fatty and high-calorie butter or dairy products.

Plant-based foods, on the other hand, are usually low in fat and calories and have a high proportion of fiber. That's why vegan dishes are usually more filling. So you have to eat less to be full. The consequence (if vegan burgers or vegan currywurst are avoided): Vegans therefore have a lower risk of obesity than meat eaters. In addition, the dietary fibers also have a positive influence on digestion and calm the intestines, which can have a positive effect on our general well-being and ensure a good mood.

So if you want to lose weight in a vegan and healthy way, we would like to give you the following tips:

Sweating instead of sitting

A healthy vegan diet is one thing, regular exercise and sport are another. If you want to burn body fat, you should also increase your calorie consumption, i.e. do sports. At least 30 minutes a day not only have a positive effect on body weight, muscles and blood lipid levels. Exercise in the fresh air also gets the brain cells going. And best of all: When the sun is shining, you also collect important vitamin D at the same time. If you consciously want to lose weight, you should consume around 300–500 kcal less per day than you burned. Various apps, for example, help you count and calculate calories.

Eating a lot is not measured

Losing weight healthily does not just mean doing without fats such as meat and butter. Of course, you also have to make sure that you eat a balanced diet in order to absorb all the important minerals, vitamins and nutrients possible. The vegan kitchen offers just about everything: Vegetables, fruit and whole grain products are just as much a part of the daily menu as legumes, nuts, seeds and soy products. The more varied you eat, the better.

Even at the stove is never wrong

If you are vegan, you should cook for yourself as often as possible and use unprocessed food as much as possible. Because even vegan ready meals are often characterized by the fact that they contain a relatively large amount of fat or sugar, which enhance the taste. The calories you consume as a result are often correspondingly high. Apart from that, many important vitamins and minerals are usually lost during production.

Drink a lot and the pounds drop

For the most part, humans consist of liquid. And that needs to be constantly replenished. Especially when you are on a diet, you should drink plenty of calcium-rich water and unsweetened teas. A special effect: a stomach filled with liquid feels full. What you should also consider, a vegan diet is often very high in fiber - which is basically good. But since fiber binds water, you usually have to drink even more fluid than the normally recommended daily requirement of 1.5 liters per day. Of course, you can also use fruit or vegetable juice or a smoothie. Ideally, of course, as low in sugar and calories as possible.

A healthy snack removes pounds

So that the big cravings do not arise in the first place, a few tasty snacks can help. If you want to lose weight, you shouldn't think of chips or vegan chocolate bars, but rather use dried fruit or nibble nuts, seeds and kernels. They not only strengthen you with proteins and fiber, but also contain valuable unsaturated fatty acids and vitamins. But watch out: they are of course much higher in calories than fresh fruit.

It's never too late for a delicious diet

If you stick to these basics, your weight loss attempts should be successful relatively quickly. One or the other of you will even wonder what mountains of vegetables and legumes you can put on your plate and still lose the pounds. But the best thing about the vegan diet: You are not only doing something good for yourself, but also for animals and the environment.

As many friends confirm to us, the vegan diet is also preferable to other diets for reasons of taste. The huge range of vegan cookbooks, foods and restaurants now offers such a breadth of taste experiences and sometimes exotic flavors that a vegan diet never gets boring and has something to offer for everyone.

Lightning Source UK Ltd.
Milton Keynes UK
UKHW021027110321
380160UK00001B/29